AVNEET
THE PO[...]
INDIAN TV
ACTRESS

SUSHANT MASIH

Copyright © Sushant Masih
All Rights Reserved.

This book has been published with all efforts taken to make the material error-free after the consent of the author. However, the author and the publisher do not assume and hereby disclaim any liability to any party for any loss, damage, or disruption caused by errors or omissions, whether such errors or omissions result from negligence, accident, or any other cause.

While every effort has been made to avoid any mistake or omission, this publication is being sold on the condition and understanding that neither the author nor the publishers or printers would be liable in any manner to any person by reason of any mistake or omission in this publication or for any action taken or omitted to be taken or advice rendered or accepted on the basis of this work. For any defect in printing or binding the publishers will be liable only to replace the defective copy by another copy of this work then available.

Contents

1. Chapter 1   1

CHAPTER ONE

Avneet Kaur is a popular Indian TV actress, dancer, model, and YouTuber. She first tasted fame as a dancer, participating in multiple dance reality shows before progressing to make a bigger name for herself as an actor.

AVNEET KAUR - THE POPULAR INDIAN TV ACTRESS

Avneet Kaur Biography

Avneet Kaur belongs to a Punjabi family. She was born on 13 October 2001 to Amandeep Nandra and Sonia Nandra and hails from Jalandhar, Punjab, India. She also has an elder brother, Jaijeet Singh.

Avneet went to Police DAV Public School in Jalandhar and currently studies at Oxford Public School, Mumbai. As for her relationship status, it is yet to be revealed; however, there have been rumours of her dating Siddharth Nigam.

Avneet Kaur dance career
Avneet Kaur began her career with Dance India Dance Li'l Masters where she was among the top three contestants. She also contested in Dance Ke Superstars and participated in Jhalak Dikhhla Jaa 5 in

2012.

Avneet Kaur acting career

Avneet Kaur had previously appeared in a 2011 daily soap, Meri Maa, where she played a character called Jhilmil. Following that, she portrayed a fun-loving and intelligent girl on SAB TV's Tedhe Hain Par Tere Mere Hain. She has also been a part of Zee5's web-series Babbar ka Tabbar. The actor has also featured in Hamari Sister Didi as Khushi.

Avneet was also seen in TV drama show Savitri, where she portrayed a young Rajkumari Damyanti. In 2013 Avneet Kaur played a young pakhi in family- drama Ek Mutthi Aasmaan. She has also received nominations for Zee Rishtey Award for favourite daughter and sister.

Avneet Kaur movies
After appearing in several TV shows, the actress gained mainstream recognition when she was cast as a child actor in the 2014 Rani Mukerji-starrer Mardaani with the role of Meera. She also featured in the sequel, Mardaani 2, which came out in 2019. The actress was widely appreciated for her performance in the films. She has also featured in a 2017 romantic-comedy film, Qarib Qarib Singlle, starring Irrfan Khan and Parvathy Thiruvothu in the lead.

Avneet Kaur is also a singer
Besides her dance and acting career, Avneet career, Avneet Kaur is also a singer and appears in music videos as well. Some of her working credits include Kaali Meri Gaadi, Taanashah, Main Fir Nai Auna, Teri Naar, Attachment, Mere Naina, Pahadan, Yaari and Tarse Ye Naina. Her songs are available for download on Gaana.com.

Avneet Kaur net worth

According to sources, Avneet Kaur has a net worth that stands at an estimated ?50 lakhs as of 2018. While her current worth has not been disclosed, it is safe to believe that the figure is only expected to soar as she progresses in her career.

Avneet Kaur Instagram

The young actress has also garnered millions of fans on social media. She currently has over 8.9 million followers on Instagram, and serves as a style inspiration for her fans. She always makes it a point to keep her fans in the loop with regular updates.

Avneet Kaur TikTok and YouTube
While the actress has already proved herself as an actor, she is also mostly busy making YouTube and TikTok videos. Avneet remains active on YouTube where she updates her fans on events while making videos around fashion, lifestyle, makeup tutorials, and more.

Avneet Kaur also enjoys a massive following on TikTok with 18.6 million followers. This is more than twice of that her Instagram page. She constantly posts videos on the popular video-sharing platform to give her fans a glimpse of her dance skills. The actress keeps honing her abilities.

Other hobbies

Along with her professional endeavours, Avneet Kaur also loves to take short breaks and explore the world. Again, she gives her fans major vacation goals with her constant posts. Needless to say, Avneet makes all styles and dresses look absolutely stunning on her.

AVNEET KAUR - THE POPULAR INDIAN TV ACTRESS

Ingram Content Group UK Ltd.
Milton Keynes UK
UKHW020707050623
422889UK00017B/2003